THE END OF THE
DINOSAURS

Written by Mary O'Neill
Illustrated & Designed by John Bindon

Published in 1989 by
The Hamlyn Publishing Group Limited
Michelin House, 81 Fulham Road, London SW3 6RB
© Copyright 1989 Mokum Publishing Inc.
Published in association with Vanwell Publishing Limited
U.K. edition edited by Neil Curtis Publishing Services
ISBN 0 600 56615 3
Printed in Canada

HAMLYN

About This Book

Millions of years ago our planet was home to a fascinating group of animals called dinosaurs. These creatures seem to have lived all over the world, in almost every kind of region. Dinosaurs were a very successful group of animals. They lived on earth for about 160 million years. This is longer than any other group of large land animals in history!

Today, not a single member of this great group can be found anywhere. What could have happened to them all? Some scientists think they disappeared quite suddenly. It seems that all over the world, at almost the same time, the dinosaurs were wiped out by some mysterious force. What could it have been? Solving the puzzle of the dinosaurs' death is one of the greatest detective stories of our time. People have many different ideas about what killed them off. Some ideas are as far out as outer space. Could a speeding, runaway comet have crashed into the earth, killing the dinosaurs? Other ideas are as simple as a change in weather. Could the world have just grown too cold for the dinosaurs? In this book, we'll look at these and many other ideas about what ended the Age of Dinosaurs. And we'll see how and where scientists today are finding more and more remains of these ancient creatures. Read on and find out what these discoveries tell us about the fate of the dinosaurs.

Table of Contents

Before Our Time

Scientists believe the history of the earth stretches back thousands of millions of years. Over this time, many kinds of creatures have come and gone. We may never know about some of them. But the earth sometimes gives us a glimpse of life forms from long ago.

Most of the remains that we find of ancient life are trapped in layers of rock. As time passes, new layers of rock form over the old ones. In this way, the layers of rock become a sort of calendar of the earth's past. Scientists can often tell how old something is from the layer of rock it is found in.

Naming the Past

Just as each month of the year has been given its own name, the different periods of earth's history have been given their own names. The chart on the next page shows the main periods of the earth's past.

Each of these periods was marked by great changes on earth. New kinds of animals and plants appeared. Old ones died out. Earth's **climate**, or set of weather conditions, seems to have changed from period to period. And all along, the surface of the earth had been moving. This movement continues today, although we do not usually notice it. But over millions of years, the masses of land that make up our **continents** have moved great distances!

Other things might have changed over the different periods of earth's history. Seas and oceans might once have covered lands that are now dry. Earth's **atmosphere**, the types of gases that surround the world, might have changed too. Animals living long ago might actually have breathed air that was different from today's!

Dinosaur Air

Could dinosaurs have breathed air that was different from ours? Scientists have found ancient air bubbles trapped in stones called amber. Amber is formed from the sticky resin, or sap, from trees. The air that was trapped in the resin is perfectly preserved from about eighty million years ago. Scientists studying the air measured how much oxygen it had. Oxygen is one of the gases needed to support life on earth. The scientists found that the air from eighty million years ago held a lot more oxygen! This could mean that ancient creatures' bodies didn't have to work as hard to get oxygen.

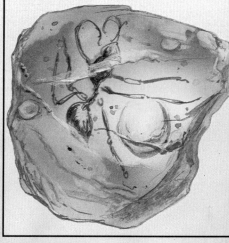

C E N O Z O I C	Quaternary PRESENT now to 40 000 years ago	
	40 000 years PLEISTOCENE to 2 million years ago	
	Tertiary PLIOCENE 2 to 7 million years ago	
	MIOCENE 7 to 26 million years ago	
	OLIGOCENE 26 to 38 million years ago	
	EOCENE 38 to 54 million years ago	
	PALAEOCENE 54 to 65 million years ago	
M E S O Z O I C	Cretaceous 65 to 136 million years ago	
	Jurassic 136 to 195 million years ago	
	Triassic 195 to 225 million years ago	
P A L A E O Z O I C	Permian 225 to 280 million years ago	
	Carboniferous 280 to 345 million years ago	
	Devonian 345 to 395 million years ago	
	Silurian 395 to 440 million years ago	
	Ordovician 440 to 500 million years ago	
	Cambrian 500 to 570 million years ago	
P R E C A M B R I A N	570 to 4500 million years ago	
	This chart is not to scale	

What's in a Name?

Scientists believe that life began 3000 - 4000 million years ago. This was during the great stretch of time known as the Precambrian (Pree-CAM-bree-un). The first creatures were single cells such as bacteria and algae. These tiny forms of life left hardly any trace of themselves. This wasn't because they were shy, but because they were small and soft!

The true record of life starts when creatures began to leave behind **fossils** of themselves. Fossils are the remains left by plants and animals. These remains can be bones, teeth, eggs, or shells. They can also be impressions or traces, such as footprints made in earth or rock.

The first real fossils go back to the **Palaeozoic** (Pay-lee-oh-ZO-ik) **Era**. Palaeozoic is Greek for "ancient life". It lasted from 570 to 225 million years ago. Both dinosaurs and **mammals** appeared in the next great era of earth's history—the **Mesozoic** (Mez-uh-ZO-ik) **Era**. This era is known as earth's "middle years" because Mesozoic is Greek for "middle life." The Mesozoic Era took place between 225 and sixty-five million years ago. We are living in the latest era of history, which is the **Cenozoic** (Sen-uh-ZO-ik) **Era**. Cenozoic is Greek for "recent life". It started about sixty-five million years ago. Many people thought that all of the dinosaurs died out before the Cenozoic Era. But as we'll see later on, not everyone agrees now!

Cones on the Seafloor

How do scientists know anything about Precambrian life? After all, Precambrian creatures were too small to be seen without a microscope!

One way scientists have learned about Precambrian life is by studying **stromatolites** (stro-MAT-oh-lites). These are odd-looking structures left behind by the earliest kinds of plants to appear. Stromatolites look like ice-cream cones turned upside down. They first formed about 2000 million years ago when blue-green algae grew in strange spirals on the ocean floor. As these tiny plants grew together, they trapped bits of sand. Slowly, the cones formed, layer by layer. Some have grown up to 15 metres (50 ft) high!

The Age of Dinosaurs

Dinosaurs first appeared towards the end of the **Triassic** (Try-AS-sik) **Period**. The Triassic Period lasted from 225 to 195 million years ago. It is the earliest period of the Mesozoic Era. The first dinosaurs were rather small. And there weren't very many kinds of them.

Dinosaurs started to come into their own during the next stage, the **Jurassic** (Jer-AS-sik) **Period**. This lasted from 195 to 136 million years ago. Many kinds of dinosaurs appeared during the Jurassic Period, including the giant ones and the fierce hunters. But the peak of the dinosaurs' rule was during their final years. It came in the **Cretaceous** (Kreh-TAY-shus) **Period**, between 136 million and sixty-five million years ago. More kinds of dinosaurs lived during this last period of the Mesozoic Era than at any other time. But by the end of the Cretaceous Period, all the dinosaurs seemed to have died off mysteriously.

Two Families of Dinosaurs

The group of animals we call dinosaurs includes a whole range of different types. Some would have been terrifying like the monsters we see in the cinema. But some were gentle and perhaps even quite beautiful to look at. The dinosaurs were not all giants either. Some were not much bigger than a small dog.

The dinosaur group is actually made up of two main kinds. The difference lies in the way their hips were built. Some kinds of dinosaurs had hips that were like those of birds. Other kinds of dinosaurs had hips that were built like those of lizards. The bird-hipped dinosaurs are called **ornithischians** (or-nih-THISS-chee-uns). The lizard-hipped dinosaurs are called **saurischians** (sore-ISS-chee-uns).

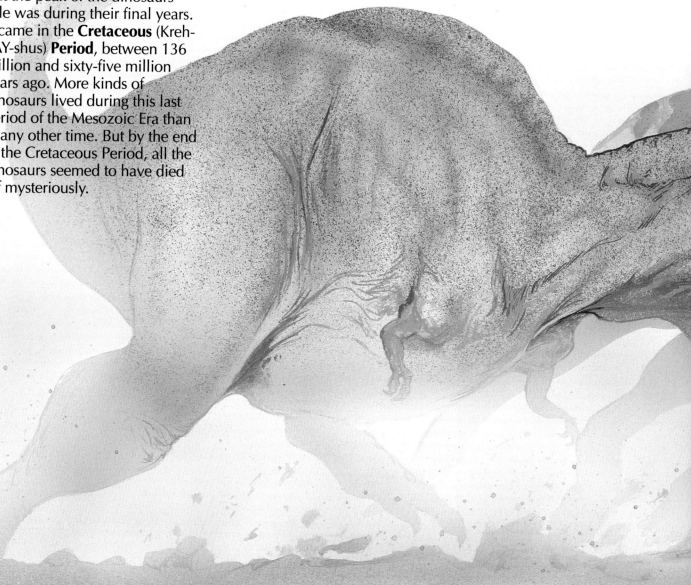

Lizard-hipped Dinosaurs

The saurischians might have had lizard-like hips, but they weren't much like their lizard cousins in other ways. The lizard-hipped dinosaurs included some of the fiercest animals that have ever lived. These were the giant meat-eaters like *Allosaurus* (AL-uh-SORE-us) and *Tyrannosaurus* (Tie-RAN-uh-SORE-us). The meat-eating dinosaurs were called **theropods** (THAIR-uh-pods).

Another group of lizard-hipped dinosaurs were the **prosauropods** (pro-SORE-uh-pods). They are thought to have been the earliest plant-eating dinosaurs. Even though they probably could choose between walking on all fours or standing on two legs, the prosauropods were probably a little awkward. Most were not very large compared to some of their later cousins. One of the smallest was little *Aristosaurus* (Ah-RIS-tuh-SORE-us). This dinosaur was just a bit larger than a big dog. Imagine standing on the roof of a three-storey building and looking into the mouth of a creature whose feet were firmly planted on the ground! Such a creature could only be one of the **sauropods** (SORE-uh-pods). This group of lizard-hipped dinosaurs included the giants, such as 27.5-metre (90-ft) *Diplodocus* (Dih-PLOD-uh-kus). You would have nothing to fear from hungry sauropods, however. They were plant-eaters and would have been more interested in munching on some tree leaves.

Another ancient lizard-hipped creature looked more like a bird. This was little *Archaeopteryx* (Ar-kee-OP-ter-ix). Its name means "ancient wing". When this creature was first found in a German mine, it was thought to be a small meat-eating dinosaur. But the rock it was found in showed prints left by wing and tail feathers! Scientists can't agree whether *Archaeopteryx* was the first bird or just an odd, feathered dinosaur.

The Bird-hipped Dinosaurs

The ornithischians arrived later than their lizard-hipped cousins. But they made up for lost time by developing into a wide and fascinating variety of dinosaurs.

All of the bird-hipped dinosaurs were plant-eaters. This may explain why some became such odd-looking creatures. They might have grown spikes, horns, bony frills, or plates to protect themselves against attacks by meat-eaters.

The Bird-footed Dinosaurs

The earliest bird-hipped dinosaurs were the ornithopods (or-NITH-uh-pods), or "bird-footed" dinosaurs, of the Late Triassic Period. These were two-legged plant-eaters which walked upright and probably used their long tails for balance. Some, such as *Fabrosaurus* (FAB-ruh-SORE-us), were quite small. This agile little dinosaur of the Late Triassic Period grew to about a metre (just over 3 ft) in length.

FABROSAURUS WAS ABOUT THE SAME SIZE AS A WOLF

Later bird-footed ornithischians included the strange "**duckbills**" and "**boneheads**". The duckbills got their name from the shape of their toothy jaws, which looked like ducks' beaks. Their jaws led people to believe that they lived by the water. Scientists later discovered that the duckbills probably spent more of their time in the woods than by the water. Besides looking a bit like ducks, these dinosaurs had unusual heads. Some duckbills had rounded crests or long tubes stretching from their heads. A duckbill named *Tsintaosaurus* (Chin-TAY-oh-SORE-us) had a horn above its eyes. This made it look a little like a unicorn!

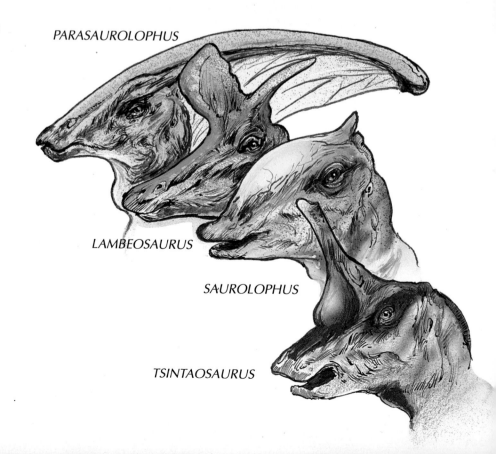

PARASAUROLOPHUS

LAMBEOSAURUS

SAUROLOPHUS

TSINTAOSAURUS

The boneheads, or pachy-cephalosaurs (pak-ee-KEF-uh-low-sores), came with built-in crash helmets. Some of these big-headed dinosaurs had skulls almost 10 centimetres (4 in) thick. They might have used these thick skulls to protect their brains during great head-bashing contests.

Four-legged Ornithischians

Other members of the bird-hipped group of dinosaurs pre-ferred to walk on four feet rather than two. These four-legged plant-eaters were heavier than their ornithopod cousins.

Meat-eaters probably stayed as far away as possible from the horned dinosaurs. These crea-tures were big, had sharp horns jutting from their heads and snouts, and might have been able to run quite quickly. Like today's rhinoceroses, the horned dinosaurs might have lowered their heads and charged at their enemies.

The **stegosaurs** (STEG-uh-sores) and **ankylosaurs** (ang-KILE-uh-sores) wore armour. The *stegosaurs* had a row of large tri-angular plates down their spines. Besides making the stegosaur an awkward mouthful for a meat-eater, the plates might have been used to catch the sun's rays. Any meat-eater that wasn't put off by a stegosaur's plates might have received a mighty blow from the stegosaur's spiky tail.

PACHYCEPHALOSAURUS

STYRACOSAURUS

The ankylosaurs were covered almost completely in tough plates. When threatened, an ankylosaur might not have wasted much energy—it might just have sat down! Its plate-cov-ered body would have been tough for any meat-eater to bite through. And its tail ended in a huge bony club that could have been swung as a weapon.

TRICERATOPS

ANKYLOSAURUS

The End of the Line

Suddenly, it all ended. Just when it seemed that the Age of Dinosaurs was going full speed ahead, these amazing creatures disappeared. Sixty-five million years ago, the Cretaceous Period ended. With it went the last of the dinosaurs. But the dinosaurs were not the only animals to face doom at that time. Almost all the large animals on land and in the sea died too. So did many smaller animals and many types of plants.

Plants and animals die all the time. When whole groups of living things die out without leaving any members, that group is said to be **extinct**. Extinction (Ek-STING-shun) happens when plants or animals cannot live with some change in their surroundings.

Earth's history is full of extinctions. Sometimes, only a few groups died out. But there have been other times when many of the earth's creatures died out all at once. These are called mass extinctions. The science "detectives" who try to solve the mystery of the dinosaurs' death also study these other mass extinctions. They hope to find clues to what happened to the dinosaurs. Perhaps what killed the dinosaurs had struck before!

Gone with the Dinosaurs

Whatever killed the dinosaurs claimed other victims. Flying reptiles called **pterosaurs** (TAIR-uh-sores) took flight for the last time at the end of the Cretaceous Period. And in the seas, the long-necked **plesiosaurs** (PLEH-see-uh-sores) disappeared forever.

As the chart on the next page shows, mass extinctions have happened many times in earth's history. During these periods, almost all of the higher forms of life died out. Before the time of the dinosaurs, most of these deaths took place in the sea. This is because, until the Mesozoic Period, most creatures lived in water.

The worst extinction probably happened at the end of the Permian Period. It brought death to a whole range of sea creatures, as well as some of the first reptiles struggling to start life on land. It killed off the last of one of earth's oldest sea creatures—the strange ocean crawlers called **trilobites** (TRY-luh-bites).

Death at Sea

Trilobites were among the earliest forms of life in the seas. They first appeared almost 600 million years ago. Many different kinds of these creatures had developed over the ages. Some had a dozen eyes. Others had long spines sticking from the sides of their bodies. And still others had huge heads on small bodies. Trilobites were among the most successful types of animal ever to live. They survived through three other periods of extinction. Then they were wiped out after almost 400 million years of life!

TRILOBITES

MASS EXTINCTION CHART

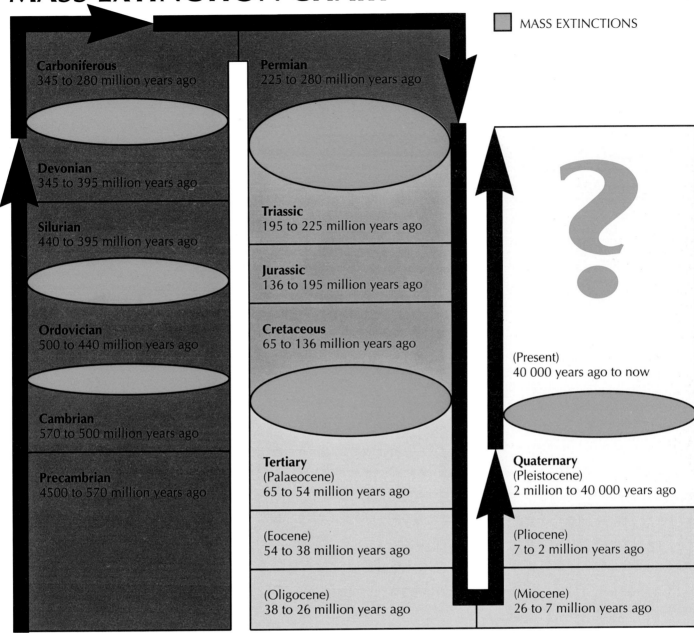

■ MASS EXTINCTIONS

Carboniferous
345 to 280 million years ago

Devonian
345 to 395 million years ago

Silurian
440 to 395 million years ago

Ordovician
500 to 440 million years ago

Cambrian
570 to 500 million years ago

Precambrian
4500 to 570 million years ago

Permian
225 to 280 million years ago

Triassic
195 to 225 million years ago

Jurassic
136 to 195 million years ago

Cretaceous
65 to 136 million years ago

Tertiary
(Palaeocene)
65 to 54 million years ago

(Eocene)
54 to 38 million years ago

(Oligocene)
38 to 26 million years ago

(Present)
40 000 years ago to now

Quaternary
(Pleistocene)
2 million to 40 000 years ago

(Pliocene)
7 to 2 million years ago

(Miocene)
26 to 7 million years ago

Another successful group of sea creatures not with us today is the **ammonites** (AM-uh-nites). These were squid-like creatures with beautiful coiled shells. The ammonites would have been a common sight in the oceans between 200 and sixty-five million years ago. Like the trilobites, the ammonites came in different shapes and sizes. Some were as small as a coin. Others were the size of a large truck's tyre. Today, we can find some distant cousins of the ammonites swimming in the seas. These are the squids, octopuses, and nautilus. The ammonites themselves died along with the dinosaurs at the end of the Cretaceous Period.

Not So Long Ago...

Closer to our own time, giant woolly mammoths and tusked mastodons roamed the earth. These and other great land mammals died out only about 40 000 years ago. Scientists think this was during an "ice age", when cold weather gripped the earth in a long, long winter.

AMMONITE

Last Days of the Dinosaurs

A cold wind blew across the plain, sending whirls of dust into the air. All around, the once green world had faded to a dull, lifeless grey. The bodies of dead and dying animals lay as far as the eye could see. Some had already withered to dry bone. The last survivors dragged themselves slowly along, searching for food and drink. But none was to be found. Soon, they would join their brothers and sisters in the dust.

Scientists don't know yet what killed the dinosaurs. But it is almost certain that some great change happened on the earth to make life impossible for these creatures. Many kinds of plants died out at that time. As plants disappeared, the plant-eaters would have followed. And with the plant-eaters gone, there would be no food for the meat-eaters.

But what mystery killer started the chain of death? We may never know for sure, but there are many interesting suspects!

The Lean Winter

Weeks had passed since the mighty hunter *Tyrannosaurus* had spotted food. Her enormous body was stiff from another night of cold. Weakened by hunger, her body was giving in to disease. Her gums were cracked and bleeding. Flesh hung loosely on the 12-metre (40-ft) frame that had once been solid with muscle.

It was the third winter of near-freezing temperatures. The forest was almost bare. The surviving plants had been stripped by starving plant-eaters. Even *Tyrannosaurus* had nibbled on branches out of hunger. With the plant-eaters dying off, her meat supply was disappearing fast.

As she walked stiffly past a clearing, something caught *Tyrannosaurus's* eye. It was a lone *Styracosaurus* (Sty-RAK-uh-SORE-us). Once a magnificent horned enemy, *Styracosaurus* was also sick with hunger. His eyes no longer focused well, but he smelled the hunter nearby. *Styracosaurus* bristled with fear.

Tyrannosaurus turned to charge at this horned meal. But with almost her first step, her knees buckled. The meat-eater's huge head hit the earth with enough force to knock her out. She would not rise again. *Styracosaurus* just stared. Saved for now, he knew his death would come soon as well.

Colder and Colder Weather

One of the most popular theories about the death of the dinosaurs is that the world just grew too cold for them. Indeed, for large, **cold-blooded** creatures, even a few nights of cold could spell death.

How could the weather have changed? Scientists think there might have been a cooling in the earth's atmosphere during the Late Cretaceous Period. The continents had also been drifting outwards towards the North and South Poles. Temperatures are cooler at the poles. Also, the shifts of the earth's surface might have upset the climate. New weather patterns might have meant bad storms and cold temperatures on earth.

The colder weather might have attacked the plants first. As they died off, the plant-eating dinosaurs would have starved to death. And without the plant-eaters for food, the meat-eating dinosaurs would have been the next to die.

Cold-weather Dinosaurs?

Not everyone agrees that a change in weather would have been enough to kill the dinosaurs. Some scientists say that dinosaurs might have been **warm-blooded**. Warm-blooded animals are able to make their own body heat. They can live in much colder climates than cold-blooded animals.

Other scientists ask why the dinosaurs could not just have adapted to the cold weather. The climate changed often during the earth's history. Many kinds of animals develop ways to live with changes in temperature over time.

Were some kinds of dinosaurs used to living in cold, dark regions? A number of scientists think so. Fossils have been found that show dinosaurs might have lived as far north as Alaska, and as far south as Antarctica. Some of these animals might have had special features, such as keen eyes, to deal with the long winter nights.

A Deadly Crash

Hypacrosaurus (High-PAK-ruh-SORE-us) looked up from the fallen tree he was busy stripping of leaves. Something in the sky had caught his attention. Above the tops of the tallest trees, a ball of light was streaking across the sky.

The duckbill stiffened with alarm. The ball was the colour of fire! He watched in alarm as it fell towards earth, even though it was many kilometres away.

Seconds later, the earth shuddered from a tremendous blow. The air clapped as if from thunder. The ball had struck!

The blow startled the rest of the duckbill herd. All heads turned in the direction of the crash. Already, a huge cloud of dust was rising in the air. Like dark fingers reaching for the sun, the dust climbed higer and higher until the sky turned black. All the while, the earth kept shaking.

In terror, the *Hypacrosaurus* herd ran in every direction, stumbling over each other. Other creatures, large and small, took flight as well. Hunter and hunted were too frightened to notice one another. The forest came alive with panic. Within minutes, the day had turned into a deadly night that would never end for the dinosaurs.

The Mystery Clay

In the late 1970s, a man named Walter Alvarez was studying the layer of rock that marks the end of the Age of Dinosaurs. He made a puzzling discovery. Alvarez found a layer of clay that seemed to date back to the time of the dinosaurs' extinction.

Where could this clay have come from? Could it be a clue to the dinosaurs' death?

Alvarez and his father Luis studied the clay closely. They found it contained a great deal of a metal called **iridium** (ih-RID-ee-um). This metal is only found in the earth's core, or in comets and asteroids from outer space.

Other scientists in different parts of the world found this iridium-rich clay in the same layer as Alvarez. Could volcanoes have spit up large amounts of iridium from the earth's core? Alvarez and others didn't think so. There was just too much iridium over too much land.

Killer from Outer Space?

Alvarez looked to the skies for an explanation. He came up with the theory that a large asteroid from outer space must have hit the earth sixty-five million years ago. The crash would have sent great clouds of dust—and iridium—into the air. This roof of dust might have hung in the air for months. It would have blocked out sunlight and may have changed earth's temperatures in strange ways.

Without sunlight, plants would not have been able to grow. With the plants gone, many other forms of life would have starved. A horrible chain of death would have brought down one mighty animal after another, on land and in water.

The Survivors

If a giant crash like this did kill off the dinosaurs, how did other animals survive? Many kinds of insects, small mammals, reptiles, birds, and fish continued to live past the end of the Cretaceous Period. How did they manage?

Some animals can wait out a disaster better than others. Small, slow-moving animals such as turtles and crocodiles can go for longer periods without food than large, active animals. Some sea animals live on types of plants that don't need much sunlight. And you've probably noticed how small mammals such as squirrels get through a long winter—they **hibernate**, or sleep through it. Some of these small animals, along with birds, can also get by on berries, nuts, and seeds. These foods can be found even when the plants that made them have died.

If it was a great dust cloud from a mighty crash that killed off the dinosaurs, the dust would have fallen to earth sooner or later. As it settled, the sun would have shone through again. And small green plants would have sprouted from seeds buried under the new top layer of earth.

Regular Crashes?

Alvarez's theory of a killer from outer space was very popular. It excited the imaginations of many other scientists. Not everyone agreed with the theory. But some scientists did agree, and they thought it might explain more than just the dinosaurs' death. They began to wonder if deadly crashes might happen often in the earth's history. Perhaps other extinctions have been caused by space objects hitting Earth!

Space Intruder

Far off, at the edge of our solar system, the family of comets waits. It has been many millions of years since their orbit was last disturbed by an intruder. By now, they have fallen into a regular pattern of movement once again. But soon, the intruder will return.

As it comes closer, its pull becomes stronger and stronger. The comets grow unsettled. Even from millions of kilometres away, they can feel the intruder's force. Thousands of years pass, but these are like days to the comets. As the intruder draws nearer, the comets on the edge of the group are pulled away. The bonds with the group are broken. They can't resist the strength of the intruding object.

Thousands of comets are swept along with the intruder. They will ride with it on its path through space. They are taken closer to planets than they have ever been before. For some comets, the pull of a planet proves stronger than what holds them to the intruder. They break away from its force and fall towards the planet.

Some comets are drawn to Mars, some to Uranus, and some to Neptune. Other comets rain down upon Earth. It has been expecting them. They have come before and will come again.

Did all this happen? Could all this happen again? No one knows for certain. Still, if such a space intruder exists, the question remains — what is it? It's a question scientists have developed at least two theories for. One is the "Death Star" theory. The other is the "Planet X" theory. Both involve the "Oort Cloud".

Oort Cloud

Most space objects such as asteroids don't hit the earth on any kind of schedule. But comets, such as Halley's comet, travel through space on a steady orbit, or path. We can guess where they will be at a certain time. They move like clockwork on their course through the skies. Comets are large chunks of ice and raw metal. One of the metals they carry is iridium.

Scientists have discovered a

huge group of comets that travel on the edge of our solar system. They have called this group the "Oort Cloud". Usually, these comets are stable and far away. Still, something could come along to upset the Oort Cloud on a regular schedule of many millions of years. This might send comets speeding toward earth. What could the intruder be?

Death Star

A scientist named Richard Muller thinks that our sun might have a hidden "twin". He has called this twin "Nemesis", but others call it the "Death Star". Muller thinks the sun's twin is a cool star that doesn't give off much light. This would explain why scientists haven't spotted it yet.

Muller believes it is Nemesis that upsets the Oort Cloud on a regular schedule. He thinks that Nemesis travels on an orbit that takes it past the Oort Cloud. If so, the Death Star's visit would disturb the comet group, sending a deadly shower towards earth. But other people have different ideas about what the space intruder might be.

Terror of Planet X

We know of nine planets in our solar system: Mercury, Venus, Earth, Mars, Jupiter, Saturn, Uranus, Neptune, and Pluto. Some people who study the universe are busy looking for a tenth planet in our solar system. They believe this mystery planet exists because something strange seems to affect the path of the planets Uranus and Neptune. They have nicknamed the missing world "Planet X".

These scientists think that on its own strange route through the heavens, Planet X races through the Oort Cloud. Could it be Planet X that sets those comets into motion?

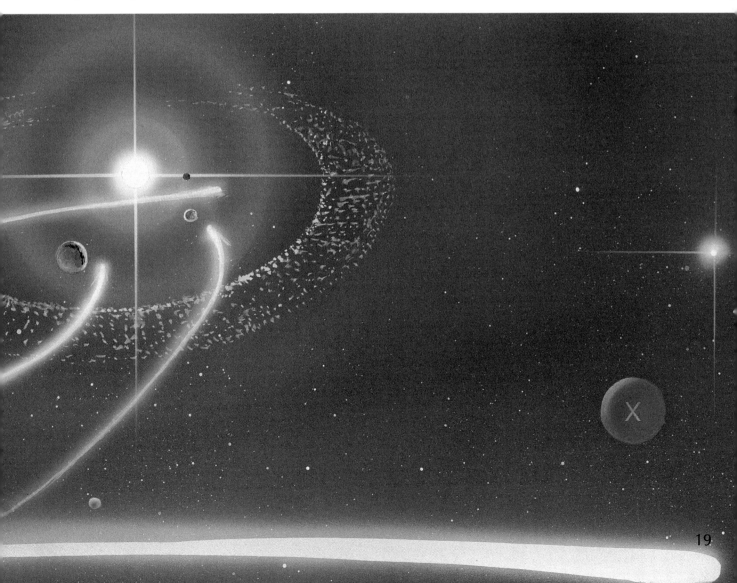

Dinosaur Survivors

The small meat-eater waited quietly behind the large spruce tree. He watched closely as a small nose appeared at the opening of the burrow in front of him. The nose sniffed the air, checking for enemies. The meat-eater was downwind, however. He could not be smelled.

Timidly, the little mammal stepped out of his burrow. He was a furry creature, not much bigger than a rat. The meat-eater pounced. Before the mammal could so much as squeak, he was snapped up in the dinosaur's powerful jaws.

With quick bites, the meat-eater finished his snack. But he could not stop to rest after that. He would need many more of these little creatures to keep his strength up. The days of large kills were long gone for his kind.

For thousands of years now, the surviving dinosaurs had lived like this—always on the hunt. The large prey had disappeared, so these dinosaurs now lived on their small neighbours. Survival was a daily battle that they would soon lose.

Was the End so Sudden?

The idea of a great asteroid or comet crash is fascinating. But it would mean the dinosaurs would all have been killed within a very short time—perhaps over a few months or years. What if the dinosaurs did not die out so quickly?

Many scientists don't think the end was so sudden. Some think that the dinosaurs had started to die off millions of years before the end of the Cretaceous Period. And even more amazing, fossils have been found in the United States and southern China that might show dinosaurs lived long after they were supposed to have disappeared!

In Montana, located in the north-western United States, dinosaur fossils have been found in a layer of rock that dates back to around 40 000 years after the end of the Cretaceous Period. And the fossils in southern China show that dinosaurs might have survived longest in that area. They were found in a layer from almost a million years after the last dinosaur was supposed to have died.

END OF
CRETACEOUS PERIOD

BEGINNING OF
CENOZOIC ERA

Dating the Fossils

Perhaps the earth is playing tricks on us. Some scientists don't agree that these fossils are really from "younger" dinosaurs. They think the fossils might somehow have moved from one layer of rock to another. Remember that the earth's layers build one on top of the other.

The "youngest" layers are on top. Could fossils formed in a lower layer have somehow been mixed up with fossils in a layer higher up?

The scientists who discovered the Montana fossils don't think so. They say that if the dinosaur fossils got mixed up with a later layer, then other Cretaceous animals should be mixed in too. But so far, only the dinosaur fossils seem out of time.

Scientists will have to do a lot more digging before we can be sure exactly when the last of the dinosaurs walked the earth. But these new finds might mean that the dinosaurs' killer worked much more slowly than we thought before.

The Spreading Illness

Triceratops (Try-KAIR-uh-tops) was in a daze. Surrounded by lush ferns and her favourite cone-bearing trees, she had no appetite. She felt hot and tired, and she could barely drag herself to the waterside for another drink. She and the rest of the herd had been ill since they had arrived almost two months ago. Many had already died. They had come to this new land after many bad seasons at home. One year had brought floods; the next was bone-dry. Each time the food disappeared, they had moved on.

The new forest seemed like a paradise at first. There was plenty of food and water, and the weather was fair. Many other animals had come to this forest from far away. *Triceratops* knew some of them from her old home. But many others were strangers.

It seemed all the creatures in the forest were suffering. Smaller animals had arrived only to find that there were many new hunters waiting to eat them. And larger animals, such as *Triceratops*, found themselves growing more and more ill.

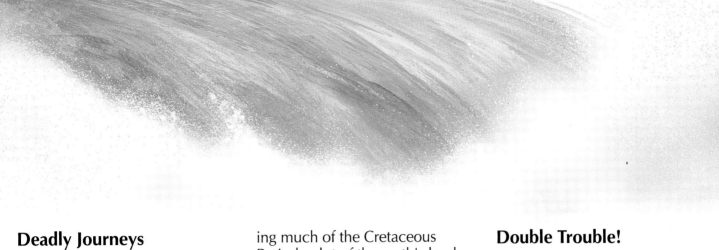

Deadly Journeys

Could the death of the dinosaurs have been caused by their moving into new areas? Illness and disease can be carried by travelling animals. Is it possible that dinosaurs and other creatures died of terrible diseases caught from other animals?

Changes long ago on the earth's surface might have joined pieces of land that were once separate. With new land links, dinosaurs and other animals might have travelled to areas they had never seen before. Away from home, they would have met up with new kinds of animals—and might have caught diseases that they had no defence against! They also might have brought diseases with them that their new neighbours could not fight.

The Sinking Seas

But how could the world have changed to bring all of these strange animals together? What were they doing so far from home? Scientists think that dur-

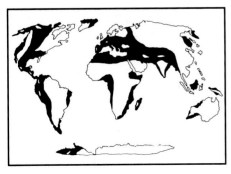

ing much of the Cretaceous Period, a lot of the earth's land was covered by shallow seas. These seas made the air moist and the weather mild. They also separated many pieces of dry land so that different groups of animals were kept apart. Living apart for millions of years, these animals grew used to different kinds of germs.

But what if these seas drained off into the oceans? The animals that lived in the shallow seas would have died as their homes dried up. Also, the deep ocean would have changed as it mixed with the water from the shallow seas. The warmer, shallow seawater would have changed the temperature of the deeper oceans. So animals living in the ocean might have died too.

Back on dry land, the home of such animals as the dinosaurs would have become cooler and drier as the seas drained off. At certain times, animals living on the lowlands might have been hit by terrible floods as the seas headed toward the ocean.

As parts of land once covered by water became dry, new travel routes opened up. With nothing to stand in their way, dinosaurs and other land animals probably roamed into new areas. There, they would have met new neighbours. And some may have brought deadly diseases with them.

Double Trouble!

If this was what ended the dinosaurs, what do we make of Alvarez's mystery clay? Does this mean there was no asteroid or comet crash? Some scientists think the dinosaurs might have been affected by such an outer space object, but only when they were already in trouble. Ill and dying, the dinosaurs might have looked up to see a fiery ball falling from the sky. If so, it might just have sealed the dinosaurs' fate.

When People Travel

Although you can't see them, germs are everywhere. And many cause disease. In different parts of the world, people get used to some of the germs around them. Their bodies develop ways to defend against these germs. But newcomers often don't have any defence against them. They may become ill and even die from diseases caused by these germs.

If you've ever travelled far away to a different country, you might have received a vaccination first. It's meant to protect you from foreign germs. The dinosaurs weren't as lucky. They didn't have any vaccinations to protect them when they travelled.

How We Found the Dinosaurs

One day, an Englishwoman named Mary Ann Mantell was walking along a road when she spotted a large tooth sticking out of some rock. Looking more closely, she found even more of the strange teeth trapped in the rock. Her husband, Doctor Gideon Mantell, said that the teeth came from a huge extinct reptile. He called this creature *Iguanodon* (Ig-WAN-oh-don)

because its teeth were like those of an iguana, a kind of lizard. The first dinosaur had been named!

Large bones had been found many times before. People used to think that they belonged to a race of giants from a long time ago. But people could not imagine a group of animals as old as the dinosaurs. Even when the Mantells discovered *Iguanodon* in 1822, they did not recognize it as a completely different type of animal from those alive today. The name dinosaur wasn't invented until 1842. It means "terrible lizard".

MARY ANN MANTELL

DR GIDEON MANTELL

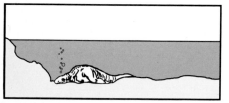

A DEAD DINOSAUR ON A RIVERBED.

THE DINOSAUR'S FLESH DECAYS, LEAVING BONE.

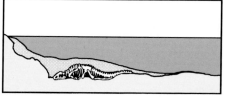

SAND AND SILT COVER THE DINOSAUR.

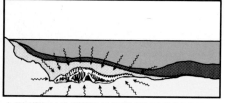

MINERALS SEEP INTO THE BONES, MAKING THEM HARD AS ROCK.

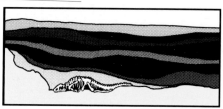

AS LAYERS OF SEDIMENT PILE UP ON TOP OF THE DINOSAUR, IT KEEPS ITS SHAPE.

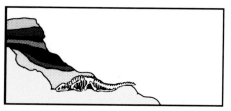

WIND AND WATER MAY WEAR ROCK AWAY ENOUGH TO EXPOSE THE BONES.

Secrets from Long Ago

Most of what we know about dinosaurs and other life from long ago comes from the fossils they leave behind. Fossils can be bones, teeth, eggs, or footprints. More rarely, they can be the soft parts of plants and animals.

Animal fossils can be made in a few different ways. When an animal dies, usually the soft parts of its body rot. This leaves behind the teeth and bones. These may be covered over by

sand or silt. This cuts off the air from the bones and stops them from rotting. As many years pass, minerals from the earth seep into the millions of little holes in each bone. These minerals make the bones hard so they are able to keep their shape as tonnes of sediment pile up on top of them. As thousands of years pass, the bones themselves turn to rock.

Other types of fossils, called cast fossils, are formed when the bones dissolve in the rock. These leave behind an imprint of their

shape. Plants often make cast fossils.

But how do scientists know where to find fossils if they are buried far down in the earth? The earth's layers don't build up evenly. As new layers are forming in some areas, old ones might be wearing away in others. Rock can be worn away by water or wind. After many years, enough rock can be worn away to reveal hidden treasures such as dinosaur bones!

Putting the Pieces Together Again

Fossil hunters rarely find whole dinosaur skeletons. The bones are usually all jumbled up. Many different dinosaurs might be found mixed together. Sometimes, most of the parts are gone. The more parts that are missing, the more difficult it is for scientists to rebuild a dinosaur skeleton.

The fossils may be scattered over a wide area. Once they are found, they have to be taken out of their beds of solid rock. Fossil hunters have to be very careful not to damage the bones as they are removed.

At the place where they are dug up, each piece of bone is numbered. People take photographs of exactly how the bones were found. The fossils are then packed in plaster to protect them from damage. Then they are sent to a museum or other place to be rebuilt. Rebuilding a dinosaur can take years! Some types of dinosaurs are never completely rebuilt. We have to imagine what they were like from just a few pieces of bone.

Earth—The Layer Cake

The next time you pass a cliff or some other place where a deep cut has been made in the earth, look closely. You might be able to spot some of the different layers. Do they have different colours? If you can, feel some of the rock from the different layers. Is some rock hard and some soft? How do you think the layers built up?

Whole Creatures from the Past

Once in a while, scientists find whole bodies of animals from long ago. These can tell us a great deal about how these creatures looked and lived. Some insects from millions of years ago have been preserved almost perfectly. They were trapped in tree resin that turned to amber over the centuries. Giant mastodons and woolly mammoths have been found frozen in huge blocks of ice. These elephant-like creatures are over 40,000 years old. Even the dried body of a whole dinosaur has been found! This duckbill was so complete that little speckles could be seen on its skin.

An Amazing Fossil Hunt

The search for clues to ancient life never ends. Since the nineteenth century, scientists have found danger and adventure on fossil hunts around the world. Areas that hold the remains of long-gone animals are often home to living wild animals! On some trips, fossil hunters have had to travel with guns packed along with their tools.

One of the most exciting hunts of modern times took place in Mongolia. That's where Chinese and Canadian scientists joined together to search for clues that might tell us about the dinosaurs of Asia.

Ghosts of the Gobi Desert

The sun beats down upon the hot sands of the Gobi Desert. Entire armies have died of heat and thirst trying to cross this parched land. The desert stretches without break for thousands of kilometres. Life there today is next to impossible. But its rich fossil beds show that it once teemed with life of the most amazing kind.

In 1987, a team of Chinese and Canadian scientists began the first stage of a great hunt for fossils in the Gobi Desert. The fossils of this region cover almost the whole life span of the dinosaurs, from the Late Triassic to the Late Cretaceous Periods. Some of the most exciting finds date from a section of the Late

Jurassic Period. These are the first fossils ever found from this period.

In trucks brought in by cargo planes, the scientists drove thousands of kilometres across the Gobi Desert. Their search uncovered a new meat-eating giant named *Jiangjunmiaosaurus* (Jee-ang-JUN-meow-SORE-us). Another new dinosaur they found was a 27.5-metre-long (90-ft) plant-eater.

The Gobi adventure included a 5000-kilometre (3000-mile) trek across the desert into Inner Mongolia. Along the way, the fossil hunters found a much older route. On it were the footprints of four different kinds of dinosaurs. What enormous hitchhikers these would have been!

The Search for Distant Cousins

The Chinese and Canadian team were hoping to find more than just new types of dinosaurs. Another goal was to find proof that dinosaurs might have migrated between Asia and North America. This might show that these dinosaurs were once related. Finding these clues might also help scientists explain why the dinosaurs finally disappeared.

Go on Your Own Fossil Hunt!

You don't have to be a scientist to find things from long ago. All you need is a patch of ground and a shovel. Pick a place where you can get permission to dig a hole. Dig down at least 60 centimetres (2 ft). Put aside all the objects you find, including interesting rocks, shells, tin cans, and other scrap. Divide your treasures into groups. Were any objects once living things? Try to guess how old some of the objects are. What does each thing tell you about what once might have happened on that spot?

Seven-Year-Old Fossil Hunter

Young Thad Williams made a lucky strike near Fort Worth, Texas, USA, in the summer of 1988. While out walking along a creek with his father, Thad saw some teeth in the ground. The teeth turned out to be part of a whole dinosaur jawbone!

Thad's father, a biology teacher, called a local museum to come and look at their find. The museum officials were amazed to discover that the fossils were from a dinosaur named *Tenontosaurus* (Ten-ON-tuh-SORE-us). It was a 6-metre-long (20-ft), 900-kilo-gram (2000-lb) plant-eater that lived about 110 million years ago. More digging turned up nearly complete skeletons of three *Tenontosaurus* dinosaurs buried there. What a great discovery for Thad Williams, who was just seven years old at the time!

Dinosaur Finds Around the World

Dinosaur remains have been found on almost every continent in the world. Some areas of the world reveal more fossils than others. Weather and other conditions in these areas have worn away layers of rock. This has brought fossils to the surface. And not all of them come from the same period in history. Some parts of the earth have worn away to show very old fossils. Other regions show us dinosaur life from just before the great extinction took place.

The map on these pages shows the dinosaur discoveries you have read about in this book. It also tells you where other dinosaurs have been found. As you can see, a number of different dinosaurs have been discovered so far. But scientists feel that many more are waiting to be discovered. One of these ancient giants might be resting in the earth below you—even as you read this!

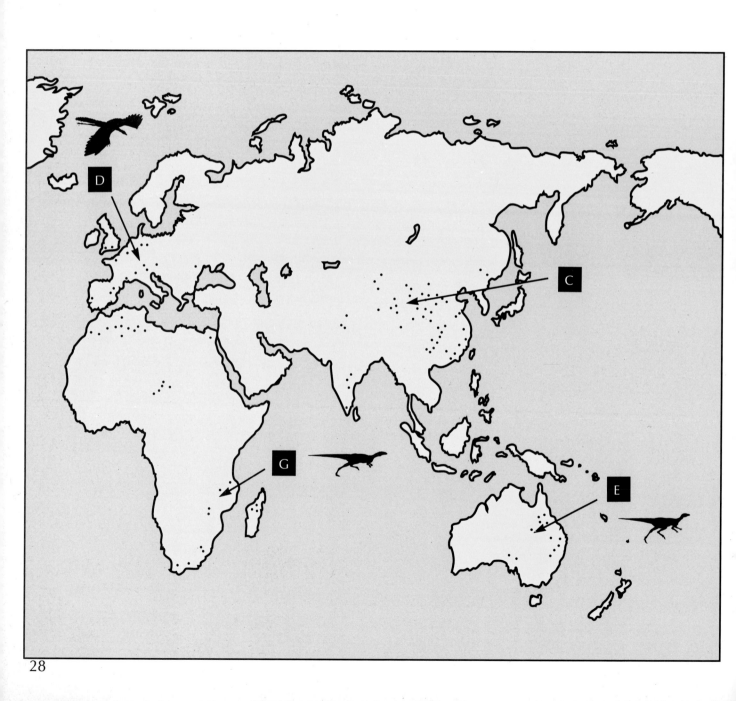

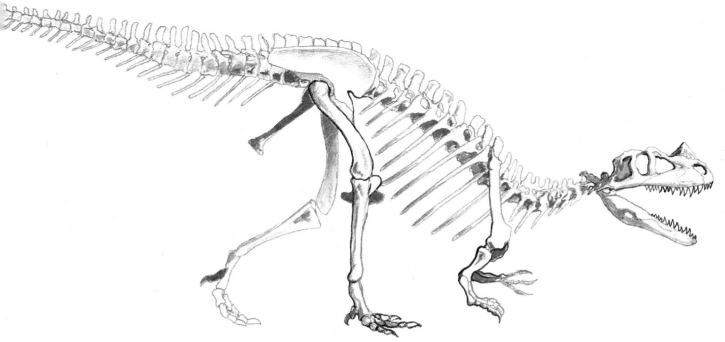

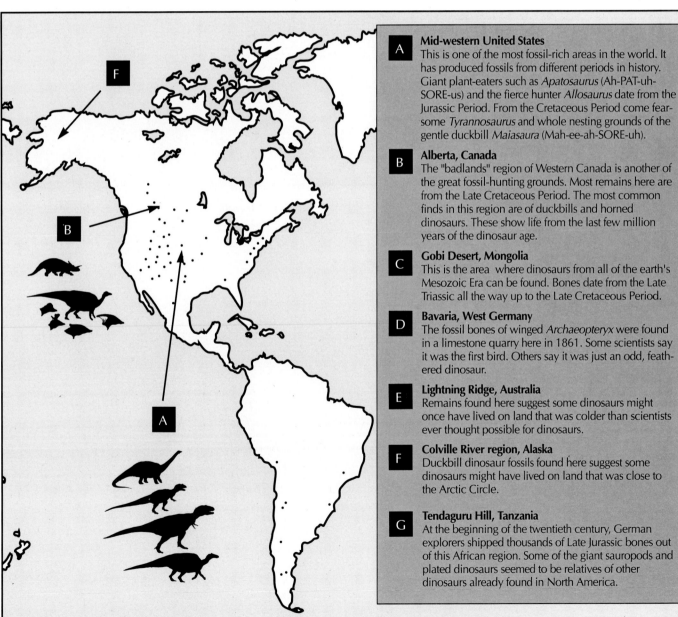

A **Mid-western United States**
This is one of the most fossil-rich areas in the world. It has produced fossils from different periods in history. Giant plant-eaters such as *Apatosaurus* (Ah-PAT-uh-SORE-us) and the fierce hunter *Allosaurus* date from the Jurassic Period. From the Cretaceous Period come fearsome *Tyrannosaurus* and whole nesting grounds of the gentle duckbill *Maiasaura* (Mah-ee-ah-SORE-uh).

B **Alberta, Canada**
The "badlands" region of Western Canada is another of the great fossil-hunting grounds. Most remains here are from the Late Cretaceous Period. The most common finds in this region are of duckbills and horned dinosaurs. These show life from the last few million years of the dinosaur age.

C **Gobi Desert, Mongolia**
This is the area where dinosaurs from all of the earth's Mesozoic Era can be found. Bones date from the Late Triassic all the way up to the Late Cretaceous Period.

D **Bavaria, West Germany**
The fossil bones of winged *Archaeopteryx* were found in a limestone quarry here in 1861. Some scientists say it was the first bird. Others say it was just an odd, feathered dinosaur.

E **Lightning Ridge, Australia**
Remains found here suggest some dinosaurs might once have lived on land that was colder than scientists ever thought possible for dinosaurs.

F **Colville River region, Alaska**
Duckbill dinosaur fossils found here suggest some dinosaurs might have lived on land that was close to the Arctic Circle.

G **Tendaguru Hill, Tanzania**
At the beginning of the twentieth century, German explorers shipped thousands of Late Jurassic bones out of this African region. Some of the giant sauropods and plated dinosaurs seemed to be relatives of other dinosaurs already found in North America.

Will We Ever Know What Happened to the Dinosaurs?

Science may never answer the most puzzling of all dinosaur questions. Fossils and other clues from the earth may not be enough to tell us what killed these mighty creatures. All we know is that, somehow, the earth changed. And it changed too quickly for the dinosaurs to survive. Imagine yourself back in the last days of the Cretaceous Period. All around, the land is littered with the bodies of fallen dinosaurs. Between the legs of those dinosaurs still standing, furry little mammals scurry. They are hunting for buried nuts and seeds. Once they would have stayed far away from the mighty dinosaurs. But already they can sense that there is nothing to fear from these dying beasts. The mammals go about their business with courage. Soon, they will rule the earth through a new age.

Glossary

ammonite Ancient coiled shell-fish; related to modern sea creatures such as squid and octopus.

ankylosaurs Group of bird-hipped dinosaurs that featured a body covering of thick armour.

atmosphere The body of gas surrounding the earth.

bonehead Common name for pachycepholosaurs, a group of dinosaurs with very thick skulls.

Cenozoic Era Earth's "recent years"; period of time from 65 million years ago to present day.

climate The year-round weather conditions of a region.

cold-blooded Endotherm; unable to produce own body heat.

continent Any of the earth's main bodies of land: Europe, Asia, Africa, America, Antarctica, or Australia.

Cretaceous Period The period of history between 136 and 65 million years ago.

duckbill Common name for the hadrosaurs, a group of dinosaurs with jaws shaped like ducks' bills.

extinct No longer existing.

fossil Plant or animal remains or impressions hardened in rock.

hibernate To be inactive for a long period of time, usually during winter.

iridium Rare, white-yellow mettallic element used as a hardening substance; found in large amounts in a layer of earth that dates back to the end of the Age of Dinosaurs.

Jurassic Period The period in history between 195 and 136 million years ago.

mammal Warm-blooded animal; feeds its young with milk.

Mesozoic Era Earth's "middle years"; period in history between 225 and 65 million years ago.

ornithischian The bird-hipped sub-order of dinosaurs.

Palaeozoic Era Period of time from about 570 million years ago to 225 million years ago.

plesiosaur Large ocean reptile of earth's middle years; resembled a large turtle with a snake-like neck.

prosauropod Oldest group of lizard-hipped dinosaurs.

pterosaur Order of flying reptiles of the Jurassic and Cretaceous Periods.

saurischian The lizard-hipped suborder of dinosaurs.

sauropod Large, plant-eating lizard-hipped group of dinosaurs.

stegosaurs Group of bird-hipped dinosaurs that featured a row of triangular plates down their spines.

stromatolites Cone-shaped structures left on the ocean floor when spirals of blue-green algae trapped bits of sand.

theropod Meat-eating group of lizard-hipped dinosaurs.

Triassic Period Period in history between 225 and 195 million years ago.

trilobite Ancient sea-crawler whose body was divided into three main sections.

warm-blooded Ectotherm; able to produce own body heat.